THE FARTS AWAKENS:
A STAR WARS PARODY

Written by
Joe Cabello

Story by
Joe Cabello
Calder Holbrook
Patrick Fisackerly
Wahab Shayek

Cover art by
Eric Owusu

Foreword by
Julian Stern

Based on
Character by George Lucas and Nickelodeon Studios

Copyright © 2015 Joe Cabello

All rights reserved.

ISBN-10: 978-1519771865
ISBN-13: 151977186X

FOREWORD
by Julian Stern

"I'm writing a foreword for Joe's Fart Awakens thing," I told my girlfriend earlier this morning.

"You mean like the scroll-y text at the beginning?"

"No, no, a *foreword*." I pointed to her copy of *Infinite Jest*, which I have not read, but have thumbed enough to know that Dave Eggers wrote the foreword. "Like Eggers wrote for *Infinite Jest*," I explained, knowing full well the absurd cockiness of my comparison.

She shook her head, quickly beginning to not care. "I thought it was a screenplay."

"It's written in screenplay *format*. But it's being printed as a *book*."

She opened her mouth, closed it, opened it again. "Why?"

"Why?"

As I write this, it is 2:34PM on Wednesday, December 9, 2015. I have just read a nearly final draft of *The Fart Awakens: A Star Wars Parody* and I know that it will be submitted for publishing sometime this evening. Joe first texted me about the idea for this project at 12:12PM on Saturday, December 5th, just four days ago.

What I am telling you, dear reader, is that this feature-length screenplay project was conceived of and almost entirely executed in *four days, two hours, and twenty-two minutes*. Completing a screenplay is a feat. Completing one in half a week is *nearly* unheard of. Completing a parody screenplay in less than five days in an attempt to release it as a book ahead of the release of the film it parodies is, to my knowledge, *actually* unheard of.

(It should be noted that this feat would have been even less feasible were it not for the story consultation from Calder Holbrook, Patrick Fisackerly, and Wahab Shayek, not to mention George Lucas, Jim Jenkins, John Kricfalusi, and the many other minds responsible for the source material for this endeavor.)

But the "Why" of *The Fart Awakens* cannot be summed up as simply, "Because it hadn't been done before." Nor can it be dismissed as a hasty scheme to capitalize on the release of one of the most anticipated films in the history of cinema.

It is both of those things, yes, but more than that, it is a product of a man who just works differently. In any sort of creative endeavor, it's easy to waste time weighing whether an idea is too stupid or too ambitious or not worth the effort. We often chalk that up to "just part of the creative process."

Well, if that were the case, you would not be holding this book in your hands because Joe Cabello skips that step every time. Why? Because, more than anybody, he knows that in doing the thing, you make it worth the effort.

There are characters named Rando Cockjizzian and Handjob Solo in this story. *Very* stupid names. But Joe doesn't worry about whether they're too stupid. He just makes sure they aren't by giving them wants and doubts and challenges and loves.

So apologies to my girlfriend, but we should never ask why someone creates. We should ask why it's so hard for the rest of us. For Joe, it's simple: do or do not; there is no why.

"If you're going to go big, go home."
-Daniel Clesi

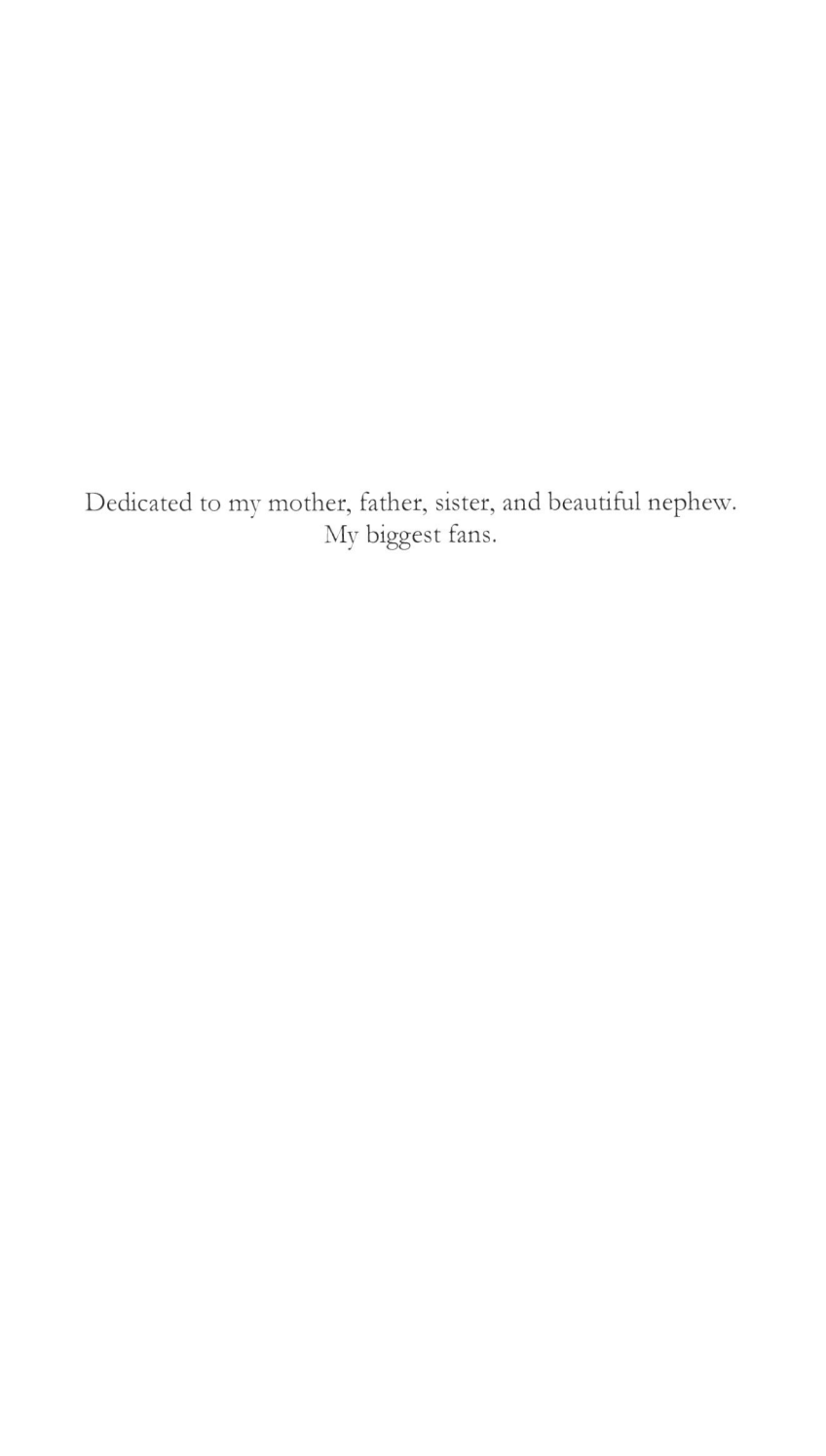

Dedicated to my mother, father, sister, and beautiful nephew.
My biggest fans.

THE FARTS AWAKENS:
A STAR WARS PARODY

BY JOE CABELLO

A title card appears on the screen:

A long time ago in a galaxy fart, fart away…

The title of our film blasts on screen with the triumphant music of Chong Williams:

THE FART AWAKENS: A STAR WARS PARODY

Scrolling text crawls up the screen on a black backdrop:

> *30 years after the fall of the Galactic Empooper by the hand of the Rebel Assliance, the Empooper has regained strength, propelled by an unknown, dark power. Lead by General Fucks, their plan to dominate the galaxy is almost complete, using a new weapon, the power of which has never been seen before.*
>
> *As time has passed and faded away, so have the lessons learned, and the heroics of the Rebel Assliance long ago. People have since forgotten the part that Luko Cockblocker played in defeating the evils of the Empooper. They have forgotten how he used the Farts, a binding, ubiquitous force found in the anus, to ultimately defeat Shart Vader.*
>
> *The Browneye, an order of warriors who used the Farts for good, have been forgotten and relegated to legend. Nothing more than stories told to children, or printed in books meant to be read on the toilet.*
>
> *There are, however, dark forces slowly gaining power, and those who have felt the farts before… will start to feel them again.*

The text disappears and we are left with the
blackness of space. It is quiet and serene,
almost beautiful if it weren't so boring, but
then-

The porcelain white of a TOILET DESTROYER, a
giant toilet, and the Empooper's most deadly and
impressive ship, floats onto the screen. Someone
has not cleaned the rim, leaving a few droplets
of splash back.

INT. TOILET DESTROYER - HALLS

The halls of the TOILET DESTROYER are white and
sterile, but everyone in sight has just a hint of
that look you make where you think you smell
something bad, but you're not totally sure,
indicating that this ship has that bathroom smell
that's kind of gross.

Marching down the halls are rows of STORMPOOPERS,
the infantry of the Empooper. Their armor is pure
white, with a toilet-lid mask, and they wield
ASSBLASTERS, laser blasters with butt-cheek
barrels.

A formation of Stormpoopers stop their march. One
Stormtrooper is next to an open door, where he
can see GENERAL FUCKS, a cunt of a man, and
CAPTAIN QRUNCH, a fat, bumbling idiot, both high
ranking officers, talking to each other.

    CAPTAIN QRUNCH
 One of the poopers has found
 something, sir. It may be what
 we've been looking for.

    GENERAL FUCKS
 Show me.

They walk off together. Our Stormpooper at the
door watches them intently. His formation moves

forward, but he doesn't fall in line - he follows
General Fucks and Captain Qrunch.

INT. DEEPER IN THE SHIP

The Stormpooper sneaks around, following the
sounds of General Fucks' voice, until he reaches
a doorway and spies.

General Fucks and Captain Qrunch hover over a
bowl of cereal.

          CAPTAIN QRUNCH
  You see, it stays crunchy, even in
  milk!

          GENERAL FUCKS
  Is this what you wanted to show me?

          CAPTAIN QRUNCH
  No, but isn't it great?

General Fucks slaps him with a rubber hand that
he always carries around with him.

          GENERAL FUCKS
  This isn't the time for cereal,
  Captain. We need to find what we're
  looking for before the weapon is
  completed. Then we can prove our
  power.

          CAPTAIN QRUNCH
  Fine, sir.
     (calling outside)
  Collins! Come in with the item!

Footsteps echo through the hall as someone
approaches. Our Stormpooper jumps into a nearby
port-o-potty basin to avoid being seen. It covers
him in poopy sludge.

COLLINS, a fellow Stormpooper, runs by and into the office. He holds something covered in a cloth.

               COLLINS
     We found this while combing the
     planet.

               GENERAL FUCKS
     The planet? Interesting.

Collins hands General Fucks the item.

Our Stormpooper climbs out of the port-o-potty and takes off his helmet. Reveal that he is none other than FINN HARDWIPER, a black Stormpooper.

General Fucks unravels the cloth to reveal…

A COLON. It is a disgusting, wrinkly cylinder, and gives off a faint brown glow at the tip, where the poopoo would come out.

Peeking around the doorway, Finn eyes the COLON in wonder.

               GENERAL FUCKS
                 (frowning)
     This isn't Shart Vader's. We must
     keep looking.

               CAPTAIN QRUNCH
     This one surely has enough farts,
     sir-

General Fucks slaps him with the rubber hand again.

               GENERAL FUCKS
        Did you find anything else?

                    COLLINS
          Some other things. Let me show you.

They leave in a hurry, forcing Finn to jump into
the basin of the port-o-potty again, but this
time without the helmet. Gross.

                    GENERAL FUCKS
          The planet Jokitch might be worth
          more to us than we even previously
          imagined, but we must continue our
          work on Naboob.

They are gone, so Finn climbs out of the port-o-
potty. He wipes the poopoo from himself,
disgusted, but then it's as if he's in a trance.
The COLON is on a desk in the room and he can't
keep his eyes off of it.

Finn walks toward the COLON as if it's guiding
him to it. His hands shake as they reach for it.
He's scared, like a young boy touching his first
boob. Scared, but excited.

He takes a deep breath, then grabs it — suddenly
he's hit with a powerful force in his body and
mind, like for just a split second he has the
answers to all the questions in the universe.
Then…

He lets out a little toot. The fart surprises
him.

                    FINN
          The Farts…

                    GENERAL FUCKS (O.S.)
          Hold it right there, thief.

General Fucks has snuck up behind him. Finn
clutches the COLON.

                    GENERAL FUCKS
          Put that down, boy.

                    FINN
          Boy?

                    GENERAL FUCKS
          That's not how I meant it. Now put
          it down.

Finn has to decide in this moment: Will he
continue obeying the orders of others and not
live his life's purpose, or will he embrace the
Farts?

He chooses Farts.

He punches General Fucks and runs down the hall.
Within an instant, alarms sound and Stormpoopers
chase after him. Brown Assblaster shots just
barely miss him.

INT. SPACESHIP DOCK

Finn ducks into the spaceship dock full of TIE
FARTERS, the standard issue ship of the Empooper.
They look like giant rolls of toilet paper. The
middle of the roll is the cockpit, and a piece of
loose paper dangles behind them like exhaust.

Finn gets into one and turns it on.

                    FINN
          Come on… Come on…

Stormpoopers enter and start shooting at his TIE
FARTER just as he gets it started and launches
out of the TOILET DESTROYER.

EXT. SPACE

His adrenaline is pumping, and he's just starting to let the feeling of victory wash over him - but a blaster shot hits his engine, sending him in a tailspin. He controls it the best he can, but-

His TIE FARTER spins out of control towards a brown planet…

EXT. JOKITCH

A sandy, desert planet.

Finn's TIE FARTER smashes into the sand of Jokitch. It's all sand and wreckage.

INT./EXT. REY'S TOILET DESTROYER - JOKITCH

A crashed TOILET DESTROYER is half embedded into the sand. It's hollowed out remains are now the home of REY TOILETBOWLER, a young and tough girl in her early 20s.

With a heavy pack full of items, she scales down the inner walls of the TOILET DESTROYER using a tampon grappling hook (unused). Following behind her is BB-69, her droid companion who looks like two giant breasts.

She reaches the bottom and unloads her haul - different toilet bowl parts. She's a toilet parts scavenger.

> REY
> Nothing good. Dammit.

EXPLOSION in the distance (Finn's crash). Rey perks up and scales to the top of the TOILET DESTROYER. She's quick, nimble, and capable.

EXT. REY'S TOILET DESTROYER - JOCKITCH

Rey reaches the top and looks out to see the settling dust of a recent crash - Finn's crash.

CUT TO:

Rey races through the desert on her SPEEDO BIKE. It's a giant, dirty speedo. She sits in the cradle of the crotch area as it inexplicably zooms through the desert towards the crash site.

INT. THE PLANETY ENDOR-GY - TREE HOUSE

The planet ENDOR-GY is home of the JIZZWOKS, a race of ~3.5' hairy bear-like creatures who live a life of constant orgies. They had been pivotal in defeating the Empooper thirty years ago, fucking all the Stormpoopers to death.

The tree house is an undulating mess of hairy bodies. Suddenly, a pale human hand bursts out from the mass of fur, covered in cum, followed by a face, also covered in cum. It's HANDJOB SOLO, aged thirty years since his adventures in the rebellion, he's now in his 60s.

> HANDJOB SOLO
> These Jizzwoks are going to suck me dry.

PRINCESS LAY-YUH, in her mid-60s, pops out of the furry mess.

> PRINCESS LAY-YUH
> Not before I do.

They kiss, obviously in love. It would be really sweet if it weren't so disgusting with the orgy of furry Jizzwoks around them.

JEWBACCA, an orthodox Jew, every inch of his body covered in payos (the curls on the side of the head of Jewish men), pops up. He's from the planet KOSHERK, as are all of his kind.

                    JEWBACCA
          I hope semen is kosher!

                    HANDJOB SOLO
          Jewie, we've been on Endor-gy for
          thirty years in this endless orgy.
          Don't you think it's a little late
          to be worrying about that?

RANDO COCKJIZZIAN, pops out from a pile of Jizzwocks. He points his fingers like guns. This is something he will always do when he talks.

                    RANDO COCKJIZZIAN
          My man!

Handjob shudders. Princess Lay-yuh pulls her finger out of his butt.

                    PRINCESS LAY-YUH
          What's wrong? I thought you liked
          butt stuff?

                    HANDJOB SOLO
          No. It's not that. Did you feel
          something? It felt like a
          disturbance in the Farts.

                    PRINCESS LAY-YUH
          The Farts? The Farts hasn't been
          around for years.

                    HANDJOB SOLO
          I've got a bad feeling about this.
          Jewie, start up the Perineum Falcon.

                    RANDO COCKJIZZIAN
                  (finger guns, as always)
              My man!

EXT. JOCKITCH DESERT - FINN'S CRASH SITE

The crash site is a complete mess. Toilet paper
wreckage everywhere. Suddenly, Finn pops out.
He's in bad shape, but ultimately safe. He spots
Rey's SPEEDO BIKE coming towards her.

Not knowing her intentions, he has to hide, but
there's nowhere to hide except… a port-o-potty.
He jumps in.

Rey parks her SPEEDO BIKE next to the wreckage
and looks around. Nothing good to salvage. Tie
Farters are all roll, no bowl. Finn peers at her
through the port-o-potty. He notices that he's
left the COLON out and she's walking right
towards it.

                    REY
                  (to herself)
              What is this?

Finn pops out.

                    FINN
              Stop!

Rey points her ASSBLASTER at him.

                    FINN
              Don't shoot! My name is Finn, and I
              just want that colon.

                    REY
              I'm Rey. Why should I let you have it?

                    FINN
          Because I need to keep it away
          from the Empooper.

                    REY
          You look like you're part of the
          Empooper. You also look covered in
          shit.

                    FINN
          I *am* covered in shit. And I *was*
          part of the Empooper. I had to
          leave. They're plotting something
          deadly. We have to stop them.

                    REY
          We?

                    FINN
          You're the only person I know and
          we don't have much time.

                    REY
          You can keep your damn colon, but
          I'm not fighting the Empooper. I
          don't get involved.

BB-69 nudges her and beeps, as if to say "you
should," but she just pushes him away.

                    FINN
          The Empooper is here. I don't know
          why, but I know they need to be
          stopped. I heard their plans.
          (beat) I can't do this alone.

                    REY
          You're going to have to.

She grabs the COLON to toss to him, but pauses
for a second. It gives her the same feeling it
gave FINN, but unlike him, she ignores it. She
tosses it to him.

He's left alone, covered in fresh shit once
again, as she speeds away.

INT. CANTINA - NIGHT

The cantina is full of aliens drinking, eating,
and smoking as a band plays. In a planet of sand
and sadness, this is actually a happy place.

Rey walks in, looking for someone. She spots the
person. It's DOUG FUNNIE, from the Nickelodeon
show *Doug*. It's normal for him to be there, and
he's her boyfriend. She sits down at his table.

>   DOUG FUNNIE
>   Hey, babe.
>
>   REY
>   Sorry I'm late.
>
>   DOUG FUNNIE
>   It's OK. I'm just happy to see
>   you.

She smiles. This is the first time we see her
show any type of happiness.

>   DOUG FUNNIE
>   Tell me about your day.
>
>   REY
>   Just did some scavenging, but
>   didn't find anything.

                    DOUG FUNNIE
          When are you going to quit that gig
          and come work with me at the poop
          plant?

                    REY
          I told you. I don't want to work at
          the poop plant. I like what I do.
          Can you drop it?

                    DOUG FUNNIE
          I'm sorry. I just care about you so
          much and want to see you happy.

                    REY
                 (unconvincing)
          I am happy.

PATTI MAYONNAISE, also from the show *Doug*, walks
in. It instantly steals Doug's attention. His
eyes turn to hearts.

                    DOUG FUNNY
          Patti Mayonnaise…

                    REY
          Fucking really, Doug?

Doug snaps out of it.

                    DOUG FUNNY
          Baby, I'm sorry. You know I can't
          help it.

                    REY
          You're such a pig!

Rey storms out.

EXT. CANTINA - NIGHT

The MUSIC from inside the cantina can be heard from the outside. Rey goes to the back of the cantina and pops a cigarette in her mouth. She can't find a lighter.

BLEEP-BLEEP. BB-69 is at her feet with a little flame coming out of his robotic nipples. She puts the cigarette to it.

>	REY
> Thanks, BB. Sometimes I think no one has my back except you.

>	BB-69
> Bleep-bleep-bloop.

>	REY
> That guy, Finn? I barely know him.

>	BB-69
> Bleep-Blap.

>	REY
> No, no, no. You're not going to get me with that "he feels the same way I do crap." (beat) Maybe I was too hard on Doug.

She finishes her cigarette. The MUSIC hasn't been playing for some time now and she barely noticed. In fact, the whole place has gone deathly silent.

She goes back to the front and enters-

INT. CANTINA - NIGHT

Everyone is dead inside. It isn't bloody, it isn't chaotic. It is as if everyone just instantly died. The only indication of anything wrong is the slight stench of farts in the room.

She runs to Doug and holds his lifeless body. She
squeezes it tight and he shudders, still holding
on to one shred of life.

He looks at her with glossy eyes-

>   DOUG FUNNIE
>   The Empooper…

His body falls still. A tear rolls down her face,
but her sadness transforms to anger.

>   REY
>   EMPOOPER!!!!

CUT TO:

EXT. JOCKITCH - NIGHT

Rey's SPEEDO BIKE barrels through the desert
towards Finn's crash site.

EXT. FINN'S CRASH SITE - NIGHT

Finn stands up as he sees Rey's SPEEDO BIKE skid
to a stop in front of him.

>   REY
>   I'm in.

He smiles.

INT. TOILET DESTROYER - CONFERENCE ROOM

General Fucks sits with Captain Qrunch on a long
table. In front of them is a hologram of
MYSTERIOUS MAN. He will always be hidden by his
cloak until his identity is revealed… if it's
revealed at all!

(it will be revealed.)

Captain Qrunch is eating cereal loudly and obnoxiously.

>   GENERAL FUCKS
> The test of the weapon went extremely well.

>   MYSTERIOUS MAN
> Good. Good. And have you found the item?

>   GENERAL FUCKS
> Not yet, master.

Captain Qrunch is eating way too loud. Mysterious Man glares at him, then raises his hand at the Captain. Captain's stomach starts to bubble and churn. He holds it in pain.

>   CAPTAIN QRUNCH
> No! No! Stop! It's not my fault it stays crunchy, even in milk!

Mysterious Man flicks his wrist and Captain Qrunch lets out a fart so big it kills him instantly.

General Fucks sits silent and uncomfortable as Mysterious Man laughs to himself.

EXT. JOCKITCH - EMPOOPER'S OUTPOST - DAY

This is a brand new outpost built by the Empooper.

Finn and Rey peer around a rock at the Empooper's outpost. There are TIE FARTERS and Stormpoopers everywhere. They are gearing up for some type of invasion.

>   REY
> So what's the plan?

                              FINN
                    Plan? I don't have one.

                              REY
                    Hm. That's ok. We can improvise. I
                    took an improv class in college.

Finn eyes her. Then-

                              FINN
                         (acting)
                    Hello Mr. Lizard Salesmen. How is
                    your wife?

                              REY
                         (acting)
                    She died of AIDS. I see you've worn
                    your cowboy hat today.

He considers the exchange.

                              FINN
                    Ok, yeah. You're pretty good.

                              REY
                    You're not so bad yourself.

Finn grips the COLON.

                              REY
                    You know how to use that thing?

                              FINN
                    Not yet.

Rey's eyes focus on something behind him.

                              REY
                    You're going to have to.

                              FINN
                    Why?-

She pushes him down as an ASSBLASTER shot just
barely misses his head. Two Stormpoopers have
spotted them.

She fires back with her ASSBLASTER and takes them
out, but another cluster of Stormpoopers are
already coming their way.

>   REY
>   Run!

They run towards her SPEEDO BIKE, but two TIE
FARTERS swoops by and destroy it.

Rey fires at the oncoming Stormpoopers while Finn
tries to get the COLON to work.

The two TIE FARTERS fly back towards them and
start firing. The blasts are coming closer and
closer to them. Rey closes his eyes and focuses
on the COLON.

>   FINN
>   Please work…

He holds the COLON out at the TIE FARTERS. Their
blasts will hit Rey and Finn any second.

Suddenly the TIE FARTERS explode.

>   FINN
>   I did it!

>   REY
>   No! Look!

Rey points to the sky and we see the PERINEUM
FALCON fly by. It looks like the Millennium
Falcon, except the cockpit is a penis head, and
the rest is a hairy mass of skin.

INT. PERINEUM FALCON

Handjob and Jewbacca man the controls while Rando and Princess Lay-yuh sit in the back.

          RANDO COCKJIZZIAN
  My man!

          HANDJOB SOLO
  We're not out of the woods yet.
  Jewie, tickle my balls.

EXT. JOCKITCH - EMPOOPER'S OUTPOST - DAY

A group of TIE FARTERS tail the PERINEUM FALCON. It fires back jizz blasts at them, but there's too many of them. It's an all-out aerial war.

          REY
  Let's help them.

          FINN
  What were you thinking?

Rey looks around at the outpost and sees something.

          REY
  Let's get them by the balls.

There's a control tower that is shaped like a cock and balls.

The PERINEUM FALCON takes heavy fire.

INT. PERINEUM FALCON

A fire starts in the back of the ship.

          HANDJOB SOLO
  Dammit! My perineum's on fire!

                    JEWBACCA
          You might want to get that checked.

Princess Lay-yuh and Rando Cockjizzian take off
their seat belts.

                    PRINCESS LAY-YUH
          Me and Rando will take care of it.
          Just keep this ship in the air.

                    HANDJOB SOLO
          Are you crazy? Sit down before you
          kill yourself.

She grabs his face.

                    PRINCESS LAY-YUH
          Let me do this. Please.

He nods.

                    RANDO COCKJIZZIAN
          My man!

She gives him a blowjob, then quickly goes off to
the back with Rando.

INT. EMPOOPER'S OUTPOST - CONTROL ROOM - DAY

Two Stormpoopers roam the hall of the control
room - Rey and Finn sneak up behind them and
knock them out.

They are now alone in the control room.

                    FINN
          If we can take out the controls,
          the TIE Farters will be useless.

                    REY
          How do you suggest we do that? I'm
          all out of assblaster rounds.

                    FINN
          How bad do you have to shit?

CUT TO:

Finn and Rey shit on the controls. The shit is so
hot and steamy that it starts to burn through the
controls.

                    FINN
          Good work… for a Lizard Salesmen.

                    REY
                    (smirk)
          Let's get outta here!

They run out.

INT. PERINEUM FALCON

The ship rocks back and forth.

                    HANDJOB SOLO
          We're losing this one, Jewie!

EXT. EMPOOPER'S OUTPOST - DAY

Finn and Rey run out of the control tower right
as it explodes.

The TIE FARTERS fall from the sky.

INT. PERINEUM FALCON/EXT. PERINEUM FALCON

They celebrate. But too soon.

A TIE FARTER falls from the sky above them and
smashes into the Perineum Falcon. The main
thruster sputters off, causing chain reaction of
explosions in the ship. It sends them into a
tailspin.

> HANDJOB SOLO
> Hold on, Lay-yuh!

The PERINEUM FALCON crashes into the sand.

Rey and Finn run to the crash and get inside the ship. It's an absolute wreck. Holes everywhere. They get to the cockpit and uncover Handjob and Jewbacca, who wake up groggy.

Handjob pushes them out of the way and stumbles into the middle of the ship.

> HANDJOB SOLO
> Rando! Lay-yuh!

Something moves to his right. It's Rando Cockjizzian. He's dying. Handjob holds him.

> HANDJOB SOLO
> Stay with me, buddy. Stay with me.

Rando's lip quivers as he looks Handjob in the eyes. He points his finger at Handjob.

> RANDO COCKJIZZIAN
> My… man…

Death takes him. Finn and Rey walk up to Handjob, unsure what to say.

> HANDJOB SOLO
> (to Finn)
> He was your father.

> FINN
> What?

Handjob doesn't explain any further. He gets up and searches the wreckage.

                    HANDJOB SOLO
          Lay-yuh!

Princess Lay-yuh is covered in wreckage.

                    PRINCESS LAY-YUH
          Handjob…

He removes the wreckage to reveal her legs are
gone. She passes out, but she's still alive.

                    REY
          The Empooper killed someone I loved
          too.

                    HANDJOB SOLO
          This wasn't just the Empooper. This
          was something worse. I can feel it.

Finn inspects the COLON. Handjob notices it and
his eyes widen. Finn clutches it closer. Is this
thing more important than he'd imagined?

                    HANDJOB SOLO
          Where the hell did you get Luko
          Cockblocker's colon?

Off Finn's shock, and Rey's "who?" face:

INT. KYLO REN&STIMPY'S SHIP

Black boots pound into the metal walkway, echoing
throughout the ship. A black cloak floats at the
heels. Heavy breathing whooshes in and out as he
walks. At his belt are two COLONS wrapped
together like a cross.

We can see his back: a tall figure in all black.

                    REN
              (hidden behind the cloak)
         Stimpy, you idiot! Will you stop
         with your breathing!

Reveal: The cloaked figure is KYLO REN&STIMPY,
the two characters from the Nickelodeon TV show,
Ren & Stimpy, Ren on top of Stimpy's shoulders.

                    STIMPY
         Sorry, Ren.

                    REN
         Just stop it with the breathing!
         Always with the breathing!

                    STIMPY
         Aw, Ren. Are you just sad because
         we haven't found Shart Vader's
         colon yet?

Ren's eyes water.

                    REN
         I just want that colon… so bad!

Stimpy reaches up to pat Ren, consoling him.

                    STIMPY
         There, there, Ren. We'll find it,
         and then we'll enjoy eating it.

Ren hits him on the head.

                    REN
         Stimpy, you idiot! We won't be
         eating the colon.

They reach a glass case.

                    STIMPY
         Oh, yeah. That's right. I forgot.

Stimpy gnaws on his foot. Ren gazes upon the contents of the case.

>   REN
>   (re: the case)
>   We are going to finish what he
>   started.

We track up the glass case to reveal what's inside - Shart Vader's busted underwear. They are soiled and have a hole in the butt from a vicious fart he suffered from.

>   REN (CONT'D)
>   We will find Shart Vader's colon,
>   and then we will get revenge on the
>   Empooper.

Ren and Stimpy drool simultaneously.

INT. TOILET DESTROYER - MEETING ROOM

General Fucks inspects a holographic blueprint. It's a planet with a butthole built onto it.

Mysterious Man appears at the doorway. His cloak covers his face.

>   MYSTERIOUS MAN
>   It seems to be coming along nicely.

General Fucks turns around quickly. He was not ready to see this mysterious man.

>   GENERAL FUCKS
>   Master. I didn't know you would be
>   here so soon.

>   MYSTERIOUS MAN
>   The time is almost upon us.

                    GENERAL FUCKS
               Yes. Tests have gone well on the
               weapon.

Mysterious Man stands before the hologram.

                    MYSTERIOUS MAN
               Ah, yes. The Death Shart.

                    GENERAL FUCKS
               We did a test on Jokitch, sir. It
               is silent, but deadly.

                    MYSTERIOUS MAN
               Good. Good.

The Mysterious Man smiles a sinister smile. The
profile of the Mysterious Man's face fades into:

EXT. JOKITCH - ADMIRAL CRAPBAR'S HOME - NIGHT

The profile of Rey. She sits on top of the
Perineum Falcon, looking out at Jokitch.

                    HANDJOB SOLO (O.S.)
               Rey. Get down here. I need you to
               meet someone.

Handjob is on the ground, near the ship sitting
at a campfire with BB-69, Jewbacca, Finn, and
ADMIRAL CRAPBAR. He's a turd shaped into a
humanoid form, with eyes, mouth, and everything,
dressed in an old, white admiral's uniform.

Rey jumps down to them.

                    HANDJOB SOLO
               This is Admiral Crapbar. He'll let
               us stay here while we figure this
               out.

Admiral Crapbar shakes her hand. It gets poop all over it.

> ADMIRAL CRAPBAR
> Ah, I see the Farts in you.

Finn looks up, interested.

> REY
> What do you know about the Farts?

> ADMIRAL CRAPBAR
> When you have fought alongside the Browneye as I have, you start to be able to spot those with the Farts.

> REY
> The Browneye aren't real.

Handjob and Admiral Crapbar exchange looks that says it all: the Farts is real.

> REY
> There were stories about what happened.

> HANDJOB SOLO
> It's true. All of it.

Admiral Crapbar nods to Handjob, knowing he is no longer needed there and walks away.

> HANDJOB SOLO
> That colon Finn has belongs to the greatest Browneye I've ever known. Luko Cockblocker.

> FINN
> Where is he?

> HANDJOB SOLO
> I haven't seen him in years.

JEWBACCA
Oy vey!

FINN
Well, the colon's mine now. We have to stop the Empooper.

REY
We're not doing anything with this pile of junk.

HANDJOB SOLO
Pile of junk? That's the Perineum Falcon.

REY
Never heard of it.

HANDJOB SOLO
You've never heard of the Perineum Falcon? It's the ship that made the Kessel Run in less than twelve parfucks.

REY
Well, now, it's wrecked.

HANDJOB SOLO
You let Crapbar worry about the ship. For now, we rest.

HANDJOB SOLO lays down next to the fire.

FINN
Rest? Why?

HANDJOB SOLO
Because tomorrow we start your Browneye training.

Finn and Rey exchange a glance – never in a million years would they imagine they'd hear those words.

EXT. NABOOB – NIGHT

Stormpoopers file out of ships on Naboob and set up camps. They are setting up a dig site.

EXT. JOKITCH – ADMIRAL CRAPBAR'S HOME – DAY

Rey's eyes peel open, awakened by the sounds of Finn swinging Luko's COLON around. Flecks of shit spray from its tip, dappling her face.

Handjob playfully kicks some sand at her.

>   HANDJOB SOLO
>   Rise and shine.

>   FINN
>   Let's do this! I'm ready to become
>   a Browneye.

>   HANDJOB SOLO
>   Cool it, Finn. We're going to need
>   Lay-yuh to train you on the Farts
>   and she's hurt bad.

>   REY
>   You don't have the Farts?

>   HANDJOB SOLO
>   Not like Lay-yuh.

>   PRINCESS LAY-YUH (O.S.)
>   You're right about that.

They turn around.

Pan down from Princess Lay-yuh's head to her legs, now replaced with plungers.

Handjob runs to her and hugs her.

                    HANDJOB SOLO
          Look at those gams!

                    JEWBACCA
          L'chaim!

                    PRINCESS LAY-YUH
          I hope you didn't think losing my
          legs would stop me.

                    FINN
          Yeah, we really did.

                    PRINCESS LAY-YUH
          Follow me.

Princess Lay-yuh walks away, her feet making a
comical suction sound with every step. Finn,
Handjob, and Jewbacca follow along.

Rey hesitates a moment, then follows.

EXT. MYSTERIOUS TRAINING CENTER - DAY

                    FINN
          Is this where we train to become
          Browneye?

                    HANDJOB SOLO
          No, kid. This is where we find out
          if you have guts.

The crew is in at the starting line of
Nickelodeon's GUTS obstacle course. It is exactly
like the 90s television show's course.

                    PRINCESS LAY-YUH
          You gotta have guts to use the Farts.

REY
          What if we fail?

Princess Lay-yuh touches Rey's cheek with her
hand.

                    PRINCESS LAY-YUH
          You won't.

It's a touching moment, destroyed by-

                    REY
          No, but really. What if I do?

                    MIKE O'MALLEY (O.S.)
          I'll be the judge of that.

MIKE O'MALLEY, the classic host of *Nickelodeon's
GUTS* and star of the hit sitcom *Mike and Molly*,
appears.

                    REY
          Mike O'malley. I thought you died
          of congenital heart disease.

                    MIKE O'MALLEY
                (with a wink)
          Not yet.
                (he blows his whistle)
          Go!

                    REY
          Huh?

Finn takes off on the course. It starts with a
tricycle hung upside down on a fixed track.

Handjob pushes her forward. It gives her the jolt
she needed to focus and she's off as well.

Handjob holds Lay-yuh close.

                    PRINCESS LAY-YUH
               Do you think she'll be OK?

                    HANDJOB SOLO
               She might not have a choice.

CUT TO:

Montage of classic *Nickelodeon's GUTS* events:

-Finn leads the way on a course where they
rollerblade upside down, but Rey gains on him.

-They go through the elastic jungle, a series of
elastic ropes cross-crossed against each other.

-Wild Wheels: on a recumbent bicycle, they race
through obstacles like uneven ground and debris.

-The Vertiboggan: a sled style event through
obstacles like broken ground, boxes, and water
cannons.

Finn comes out ahead of Rey in every event.

EXT. NICKELODEON'S GUTS - AGGRO KRAG

Finn runs up to the base of the Aggro Krag, a
giant, fake mountain, the final challenge in
Nickelodeon's GUTS.

He sees Rey running towards it and he starts to
climb.

Rey reaches the base and starts her climb. She
doesn't want to lose.

Halfway up the Aggro Krag, Rey is only fifteen
feet behind Finn, but she slips, only hanging on
by her finger tips, 200 feet in the air. Finn
looks down at her and she looks up with pleading
eyes, but he continues up.

Rey takes a deep breath and swings her other hand
up. Somehow she's come back stronger and climbs
with a flurry. She's actually gaining on him.

Finn climbs nervously, pushing himself to the
limit, but she's at his level now. Trying to beat
her he climbs too quickly and his finger misses
the ledge. He falls in slow motion with no hope
of grabbing anything… Finn is going to die… but-

Rey's hand grabs his wrist, and with all her
strength she holds on to him.

>   REY
>   Grab the ledge!

He regains footing and takes a deep breath. Close
call.

>   FINN
>   Thanks.

She can only nod at him. She would have never let
him fall. No matter what. It's just not how she's
wired.

They reach the top together where Handjob,
Jewbacca, and Lay-yuh are.

>   FINN
>   (out of breath)
>   How'd you get up here?

>   PRINCESS LAY-YUH
>   The stairs.

She points to easily accessible stairs.

>   HANDJOB SOLO
>   There's your first lesson. Always
>   take the stairs.

REY
          Is that it? I don't feel any stronger.

                    PRINCESS LAY-YUH
          No. There's one more thing. This is
          where you find the Farts.

She steps to the side to reveal the:

EXT. LEGENDS OF THE HIDDEN TEMPLE

It's the temple from the Nickelodeon show *Legends of the Hidden Temple*.

Rey and Finn walk in. It's an ancient temple covered in vine – at this point if you don't know *Legends of the Hidden Temple* or any of these references, look them up.

They reach a dead end.

                    REY
          A dead end?

Finny rubs away the vines on the wall to reveal – OLMEC'S HEAD – a Mayan statue head – the guardian of the temple.

                    OLMEC
          Hellooooooo.

Finn stumbles away scared and grabs the COLON. It ignites a gaseous blade.

                    FINN
          Whoa.

                    OLMEC
          Welcome to my temple. I remember
          that colon. That was Luko
          Cockblocker's.

                    FINN
          It's mine now.

                    OLMEC
                    (to Rey)
          And you. Where is your colon, Browneye?

                    REY
          I'm not a Browneye. I just want
          revenge on the Empooper.

                    OLMEC
          Whatever it is you seek, you will
          find it in the temple. If you're
          worthy of the Farts, the great
          master Chode-a will appear to guide
          you.

Two doorways open, and Finn and Rey walk into each one.

Olmec waits peacefully, but a bird shits on his lip.

INT. LEGENDS OF THE HIDDEN TEMPLE

Finn walks through the temple with the COLON out, revealing the gaseous blade.

He hears whispers and walks deeper.

CUT TO:

Rey walks along, pushes away cobwebs. She hears stones clack in the distance so she pulls out her ASSBLASTER.

She walks along a rickety bridge. Halfway along
it snaps. To save herself she has to drop the
ASSBLASTER to climb up. As she reaches the top
she sees something shining gold under a pile of
wood that she never would have seen if the bridge
wouldn't have broken.

Pulling herself up, she goes to the object and
grabs it. It's a piece of the GOLDEN MONKEY.

She continues along, gingerly looking for more
pieces.

She finds one in a spider web.

She sees another underwater so she dives in and
retrieves it from the bottom.

Finally she has all of them to make a complete
GOLDEN MONKEY.

Admiring her little treasure she looks up and
sees an altar with an inscription of a monkey.

At the altar she hovers the GOLDEN MONKEY over a
spot that will fit it perfectly.

>   REY
> Please. I need answers. If it's the
> Farts that will get my revenge
> against the Empooper, then that's
> what I want. I just need answers.

She takes a deep breath then plants the GOLDEN
MONKEY down.

Beat.

Nothing happens.

She does it again. This time there's a mechanical clicking and whoosh of air. Could this be Chode-a?

Nope! Balloons fall from the ceiling and that's it.

          REY
  Dammit! I hate this! I hate it!

EXT. LEGENDS OF THE HIDDEN TEMPLE

Rey comes out huffing and puffing.

          HANDJOB SOLO
  What happened?

Finn runs out, ecstatic.

          FINN
  I met him. I met Master Chode-a.

          JEWBACCA
  Mazeltov!

Princess Lay-yuh puts her hand on Rey's shoulder.

          PRINCESS LAY-YUH
  It's OK, Rey.

          REY
  I don't care. I'm ready to destroy the Empooper.

          FINN
  Come on. I think I have a plan.

Finn and Rey walk off.

Handjob and Lay-yuh watch them.

HANDJOB SOLO
             I hope they're ready.

INT. NABOOB ARCHAEOLOGICAL SITE - NIGHT

Stormpoopers comb through the underground
archaeological site. One of them hammers away at
a wall when suddenly it erupts in a gaseous
blast.

                    STORMPOOPER DIGGER
                 (in his walkie)
             Sir, we may have found something on
             Naboob.

INT. KYLO REN&STIMPY'S SHIP

Ren sleeps curled up next to Stimpy. A bubble of
snot inflates out of Stimpy's nose with every
snore.

Suddenly, Ren's eyes open wide, red with fury.

                    REN
             The colon. I can feel it!

Stimpy snorts awake for a second. Long enough to
grab Ren and crush him in a sleepy hug.

                    REN
             Let go of me, you idiot!

INT. ADMIRAL CRAPBARS SHIP

Finn stands in front of a holographic screen. It
depicts Naboob.

                    FINN
             I heard General Fucks talking about
             Naboob. I think this is where their
             secret weapon is.

                    PRINCESS LAY-YUH
          What is it?

                    FINN
          He said it was silent, but deadly.

Rey perks up.

                    REY
          Whatever killed my boyfriend was
          silent but deadly.

Finn nods gravely.

                    FINN
          We'll go in and assault them.
          They'll never see it coming.

                    HANDJOB SOLO
          How's the repairs on the Perineum
          Falcon looking, Crapbar?

                    ADMIRAL CRAPBAR
          It still needs time, but you can
          use my ship.

                    REY
          You won't be fighting with us.

                    ADMIRAL CRAPBAR
                (covering up his shame)
          I don't fight anymore.

                    HANDJOB SOLO
          Thank you, Crapbar. You've done enough.

Admiral Crapbar nods and leaves.

                    REY
          Why won't he fight?

                         HANDJOB SOLO
                    He can't help it. He's a big piece
                    of shit.

EXT. SPACE

Admiral Crapbar's ship, a giant turd, zooms
through space.

EXT. NABOOB ARCHAEOLOGICAL SITE - NIGHT

Stormpoopers busily work around the site. They
prepare a Y-WANG, a cargo ship with three pointed
wings shaped as penises.

Everyone is too busy to notice-

Our group of heroes hiding in the bushes.

                         HANDJOB SOLO
                    Jewie will make a distraction. When
                    their numbers are thin, we'll
                    attack.

Jewbacca sneaks away.

Rey moves next to Finn.

                              REY
                    What did Master Chode-a tell you.

                             FINN
                    Oh, he- uh-

                         JEWBACCA (O.S.)
                    When are you going to find yourself
                    a nice young lady?

The Stormpoopers hear Jewbacca voice behind some
bushes and follow it.

                    STORMPOOPER GROUP
          Huh?

                    HANDJOB SOLO
          Quiet, you two. It's time.

Only a few Stormpoopers are left guarding the
ship.

                    HANDJOB SOLO
          Now!

Handjob, Rey, Finn, BB-69, and Lay-yuh rush the
Stormpoopers.

The Stormpoopers get shot down quickly by Rey and
Handjob's ASSBLASTERS.

BB-69 trips them.

Princess Lay-yuh knocks one down and he falls
with his butt in the air.

                    PRINCESS LAY-YUH
          I'm going to kick your ass!

She kicks his ass, suctioning her plunger foot on
it. When she pulls it away, his entire insides
come out.

They see the unguarded entrance to the
archaeological site.

                    HANDJOB SOLO
                (to Finn)
          Do you know how to use that thing, kid?

Finn nods and ignites the gaseous blade of the
COLON. He holds it above his head for a charge
then-

EXPLOSION!!! The archaeological site is hit with
a blast.

>   HANDJOB SOLO
>   Wow. Never seen a colon do that
>   before.

>   FINN
>   It wasn't me.

A shadow casts over them. They look up to see
KYLO REN&STIMPY'S SHIP, a giant, wooden log.

It lands and the hatch opens up. Out steps Kylo
Ren&Stimpy. Ren's hand falls, holding the
combined COLONS of him and Stimpy's. It ignites
into one large gaseous stream and two smaller
streams to the side.

Stormpoopers flood out of the entrance of the
site and start blasting.

>   STIMPY
>   Let me hold it, Ren.

Stimpy tugs at the COLON. Him doing this actually
blocks one of the Stormpooper's ASSBLASTER shots.
This is how they will fight - Ren and Stimpy
bicker, inadvertently producing great fighting
moves.

As they wrestle over their colons, they deflect
blaster shots, sending them back at the
Stormpoopers.

>   REY
>   Who the hell is that?

>   FINN
>   I don't know, but he's mine.

Finn charges at Kylo Ren&Stimpy.

The others run into the archaeological site.

Finn approaches Kylo Ren&Stimpy.

>   REN
> You are no Browneye. Get out of my
> way, fool.

Finn ignites his gaseous blade and swings at them.

>   STIMPY
> I want to see.

Stimpy peers out, tossing Ren back, which dodges the attack. Finn gets in a COLON battle with them.

Ren and Stimpy fumble the COLON around, which actually make amazingly deft attacks. As they tug back and forth, it swings faster than they could possibly swing on their own. They push each other away or run into each other to dodge Finn's attacks, and their lack of balance standing on each other's shoulders makes for an incredibly difficult target.

Finn struggles to keep up.

INT. ARCHAEOLOGICAL SITE

Lay-yuh, Rey, and Handjob run through, blasting away Stormpoopers.

>   REY
> This doesn't look like a weapon.

They reach a room with a GIANT CRATE. Rey assblasts the two Stormpoopers guarding it. Another comes behind her, but Lay-yuh does the kick-disembowel with her plunger. Motherfucking girl power.

They approach the crate and remove the lid.

                PRINCESS LAY-YUH
  It can't be.

Inside is SHART VADER'S COLON. It is burst open on one side, which makes the gaseous stream even more powerful. It's wretched.

                GENERAL FUCKS (O.S.)
  Hold it right there.

General Fucks aims an ASSBLASTER at them. They know he has the drop on them so they put their weapons down.

                GENERAL FUCKS
  You fools. I'll kill you either
  way. Prepare to die.

Gulp.

Jewbacca comes from behind.

                JEWBACCA
  Be a mensch.

He knocks General Fucks out.

                PRINCESS LAY-YUH
  Let's get out of here.

They leave, but Rey stays. She looks at the colon. She's about to grab it. She wants it.

BB-69 hits her legs just as she's about to grab it, and Handjob comes back.

                HANDJOB SOLO
  You don't want that one, kid. Come
  on. Let's go!

EXT. ARCHAELOGICAL SITE - NIGHT

Finn is on the losing side of the battle against Kylo Ren&Stimpy. He's simply not ready in his training to face such a foe.

Kylo Ren&Stimply just barely miss Finn's face with their gaseous blade. The stench alone knocks him down though.

                    KYLO REN&STIMPY
          Like I said. You are no Browneye.

Finn sees the crew of heroes rush towards him. It's a circle of chaos as they surround him and blast Kylo Ren&Stimpy, but through Ren and Stimpy's loss of balance, they dodge every attack. Simply put, our entire crew is no match for Kylo Ren&Stimpy's ineptitude.

Rey's blaster gets knocked out of her hand and Handjob Solo falls on his ass.

                    KYLO REN&STIMPY
                      ("Force fart!")
               Farts Fart!

Stimpy sticks his butt out and farts at Jewbacca, Princess Lay-yuh, and Finn, toppling them over.

Kylo Ren&Stimpy walk to the fallen Handjob Solo. Rey is powerless. She has no weapon. She's frozen.

Handjob looks him dead in the eye.

                    HANDJOB SOLO
               Fart on me and I will become more
               powerful than you could possibly
               imagine-

Kylo Ren&Stimpy doesn't let him finish before he
slams his COLON down on Handjob, killing him.

          REY
  No!!!

The others are barely recovering.

          KYLO REN&STIMPY
  You idiot woman. Now it's your
  turn.

Rey stumbles back and falls. She can't get up.
She's done for…

But then – Empooper troops come in droves
blasting at Kylo Ren&Stimply.

Kylo Ren&Stimpy retreats onto his ship and blasts
away.

Our heroes recover.

          FINN
  We've gotta go.

Lay-yuh realizes Handjob is dead. She hesitates,
but she's strong. Death is no stranger to her.
She gives him one last tug on his flaccid penis,
then leaves. There will be a time for mourning.

          PRINCESS LAY-YUH
  Follow me!

They run away. Jewie sheds a tear and follows.

LATER

The ground smolders from the battle. Stormpoopers
lay everywhere.

A boot crunches down on a Stormpoopers head as it casually marches through. It belongs to the Mysterious Man.

As he walks toward the entrance of the archaeological site, a group of Stormpoopers carry the case holding Shart Vader's colon.

He waves the Stormpoopers away and gazes down at the COLON. He holds it in his hands and laughs maniacally.

A Stormpooper Helper carries General Fucks out.

>STORMPOOPER HELPER
>What should we do with General Fucks, sir?

>MYSTERIOUS MAN
>He has outlived his usefulness. Kill him.

>STORMPOOPER HELPER
>Excuse me, sir?

>MYSTERIOUS MAN
>(snapping)
>Do it!

>STORMPOOPER HELPER
>(in a trance-like state)
>Yes, sir.

The Stormpooper Helper wrings General Fucks' neck as he starts to wake up. His eyes tear up and he gasps, pleading for it to stop. Mysterious Man just gazes at him, smiling.

General Fucks dies.

                    MYSTERIOUS MAN
          Prepare my ship. We're going to the
          Death Shart. It's time.

INT. ADMIRAL CRAPBAR'S HOME - NIGHT

Admiral Crapbar consoles Princess Lay-yuh in a
far corner of the room. She's devastated, but
she's strong. She knows she needs to keep it
together.

Finny and Rey sit together.

                    FINN
          We got our asses handed to us.

                    REY
          Of course we did. They're the
          Empooper, and who the hell are we?
          Nobody.

                    FINN
          Don't talk like that. We're Browneye-

                    REY
          No we're not. A Browneye wouldn't
          have lost.

                    FINN
          A Browneye wouldn't give up either.

                    REY
          Like I said, I'm not a Browneye.

Rey grabs her jacket.

                    FINN
          What are you doing?

                    REY
          Giving up.

Princess Lay-yuh notices the commotion and comes
over to them.

>   PRINCESS LAY-YUH
>   Rey. Don't.
>
>   REY
>   The Empooper is just too powerful.
>   As long as we keep fighting,
>   they'll just kill more people we
>   care about.
>
>   FINN
>   We have to fight!
>
>   REY
>   With what? Jewbacca is sitting
>   shiva, we've got that psycho Kylo
>   Ren&Stimpy after us now, and you're
>   just some wannabe who thinks he's a
>   Browneye.
>
>   PRINCESS LAY-YUH
>   I'm no stranger to death, but take
>   it from me. You can always come
>   back from losing someone you love.
>   What you can't come back from is
>   losing yourself.
>
>   REY
>   I never asked for this. I never
>   asked to fight.
>
>   FINN
>   None of us did, especially me. All
>   I know is I used to fart for the
>   Empooper. Now I fart for myself.

She stares him in the eye. Maybe he's reached
her? But no.

                              REY
                       (shouting to Crapbar)
                  Crapbar, can I borrow an X-Wang?

He nods gravely from across the room.

                              FINN
                  You can't do this.

                              REY
                  I don't owe you anything.

Rey leaves. Finn tries to pursue but Princes Lay-yuh stops him.

                              PRINCESS LAY-YUH
                  The Farts are strong in her. She
                  just needs to find it.

INT. X-WANG - SPACE

The X-WANG is a one-person spaceship with four penis shaped wings in an X formation. BB-69 plugs into the front, also giving the ship tits.

She has no idea where she's going and she doesn't care. She just needs to get away from her old life and all the memories of the Empooper.

As she flies through space she can't help but be reminded of the destruction the Empooper is capable of. Wreckage of soiled toilet paper litters space, eerie monuments to the galaxy's fallen loved ones.

Suddenly her ship jolts and changes course. Lights flash and alarms blare. She tries to grab at the controls but there's nothing she can do to get control of the ship. The monitor reads:

Destination: Dagoballs

Her X-WANG heads straight for the little green planet of Dagoballs.

EXT. DAGOBALLS - NIGHT

The X-WANG gently sets down into a swamp then shuts down. Rey jams her finger into the ignition (a tiny butthole), but only a dribble of pre-cum drops from the cock engines. She's stuck.

She looks out at the swamp. It's dark and there's nothing out there. She resigns, kicking her feet up on the dash and folding her arms. Soon, she's asleep.

REY'S DREAM

Rey wakes up in her destroyed TOILET DESTROYER home. Doug Funnie is cooking eggs. It's as if everything is all right.

                    REY
          Doug, I thought you were dead?

                    DOUG FUNNIE
          Dead? No silly. Do I look dead to you?

He kisses her forehead.

                    DOUG FUNNIE
          Do you want some eggs?

She sighs relief and smiles.

                    REY
          Sure, I'd love some eggs.

                    DOUG FUNNIE
          No. I said, "Do you want some AIDS?"

                    REY
          What?

Doug's face starts to melt. Rey screams and
stumbles back into Handjob Solo who is also
melting.

She runs, but she's not moving anywhere. Suddenly
she's in pitch blackness and Kylo Ren&Stimpy are
behind her. No matter how fast she runs he gets
closer and closer.

Mysterious Man walks toward her from the opposite
side. They're flanking her.

>   MYSTERIOUS MAN
>   Yes. Give in to your fear. Let the
>   Farts burn inside of you.

She looks down at her gut. It bubbles with the
darkest, nastiest fart.

>   REY
>   Noooooooo!

She makes the same face Captain Qrunch made
before the death-fart took him, but before she
releases:

EXT. DAGOBALLS - DAWN

She wakes up in a cold sweat, breathing heavily.
She touches her gut to make sure everything is
ok. As she calms down she looks out and sees a
figure walking in the distance, but she can't
quite make out who it is.

She exits the ship.

EXT. FARTHER INTO DAGOBALLS - DAWN

She quietly walks through the trees and can hear
grunting. It's getting louder as she gets closer.

She comes to see the back of a small, green man who is obviously masturbating.

>   REY
>   Excuse me?

He continues, undisturbed.

>   SMALL MAN
>   Hm?

>   REY
>   What are you doing?

>   SMALL MAN
>   Masturbating, I am.

He finishes on some leaves.

>   REY
>   Disgusting.

He eats the very leaves he came on, turns around, and walks up to her. This is Master Chode-a.

>   CHODE-A
>   Chode-a, I am.

>   REY
>   *You're* Master Chode-a?

He nods happily.

>   REY
>   I'm Rey-

>   CHODE-A
>   Know who you are, I do. And what
>   you must do, I know.

>   REY
>   What must I do?

					CHODE-A
			Learn the Farts, you must. Stop the
			dark side of the Farts, you will.

					REY
			I was supposed to see you in the
			temple. Why can I see you now?

					CHODE-A
			Ready, you are.

					REY
			For what?

					CHODE-A
			To train.

INT. ADMIRAL CRAPBARS HOME - DAY

Finn practices with the COLON. His moves are
sloppy. He's still far from mastering the art.

Princess Lay-yuh watches him from a table covered
in shiva food: bagels, dried fruit, baked goods,
and chocolate. Jewbacca picks at the food, then
solemnly leaves. Princess Lay-yuh looks out the
window at the planet, the galaxy.

					PRINCESS LAY-YUH
			Rey… I hope you find what you're
			looking for…

EXT. DAGOBALLS - DAY

Rey stands in a tree above her X-WANG. A chain
hangs down from her vagina, tied to the ship.
She's trying to use her Kegel muscles to lift it
out. It proves too difficult.

                    REY
          This is impossible. Plus, I thought
          we were going to be training, not
          doing this dumb stuff.

                    CHODE-A
          Training, this is. Trust, you must.

                    REY
          I want to learn the Farts. I
          should be eating beans, or
          developing lactose intolerance.

                    CHODE-A
          Ways of the dark side of the Farts,
          you speak. The easy path, we must
          not take.

She sighs, then continues to try.

LATER

Rey stands in a clearing with Chode-a in front of
her.

                    REY
          What now?

                    CHODE-A
          Dodge, you must.

                    REY
          Dodge what?

                    CHODE-A
          My cum.

                    REY
          Hah! I'm pretty sure I'm faster
          than your cum.

He touches his penis and a string of cum shoots
out at lightning speed, hitting her in the face.

>   REY
>   Holy shit.

He laughs at her, then touches his penis again.
This time she dodges it. Then again. And again.
She dodges each one, but he doesn't let up. It
gets to a point where she can't dodge anymore and
all she can do is cover up.

>   REY
>   Stop! Stop!

He continues for a few spurts, then stops.

>   CHODE-A
>   Stop, your enemies will not.

>   REY
>   I hate them.

>   CHODE-A
>   Hate your enemies, you must not.
>   Sure way to the dark side of the
>   Farts, it is.

She wipes herself off.

>   CHODE-A
>   Kegels, we must do.

>   REY
>   I'm not doing anymore Kegels. I'm
>   not going to lift that damn thing.
>   It's too big.

                    CHODE-A
          Size matters not. Look at me. Judge
          me by my size do you?
                    (he points to his penis)
          For my ally is the Farts. And a
          strong ally it is.

                    REY
          What you want me to do is
          impossible.

Rey sits down, giving up.

Choda-a looks at her. He knows he must prove to
her, so he walks to the swamp and submerges his
butt. His face is of complete focus.

The swamp starts to bubble and it gets Rey's
attention and she stands up.

The swamp bubbles feverishly and the X-WANG
begins to rise from the swamp until it floats
completely out, held up by methane gas, and
settles back on solid ground.

                    REY
          I don't believe it.

                    CHODE-A
          That is why you are not succeeding.

Rey lets that comment settle in.

She holds her stomach.

                    REY
          I have to shit.

Chode-a grimaces. This isn't normal gas. This is
the dark side of the Farts calling to her.

CHODE-A
          Powerful is the dark side of the
          Farts. Face your fears, you must.

Chode-a points to a cave. The entrance looks like
a vagina.

                    REY
          What's in there?

Chode-a says nothing to answer this. He reaches
for something in his bag - a baseball sized glass
ball.

                    CHODE-A
          Keep this in your vagina no matter
          what, you must.

                    REY
          I'll try.

She shoves the ball in her vagina.

                    CHODE-A
          Try not. Poo, or poo not. There is
          no try.

Rey takes a deep breath and enters the cave.

INT. CAVE

Rey moves slowly through the cave. It's deathly
silent and creepy as all hell.

She reaches a corner and approaches it, but-

Kylo Ren&Stimpy comes from around the corner and
ignites his colon.

In complete terror, Rey walks backwards. The
glass ball begins to fall from her vagina. One
more step back and it will fall completely.

Kylo Ren&Stimpy swings the colon at her. She must choose to release the ball from her vagina, or be destroyed…

She closes her eyes and stands strong. The ball slides back into her vagina as his colon hits her, but-

Nothing happens.

She opens her eyes and he's gone. She sighs relief.

EXT. DAGOBALLS - DAY

Rey comes out of the cave and Chode-a smiles.

          CHODE-A
Succeeded, you have.

          REY
Who is he?

          CHODE-A
Kylo Ren&Stimpy, a master of the dark side of the Farts, but your enemy he is not. He's consumed by his hate for the Empooper.

          REY
Not my enemy?

          CHODE-A
Your enemy, seen you have not. More powerful than Kylo Ren&Stimpy, he is.

          REY
Whoever he is, I need more training. I don't think I can beat him.

CHODE-A
Defeat him, you can.

REY
But how? I don't have the Farts. I
don't even have a colon like Finn.

CHODE-A
Something much stronger than a
colon, you have.

REY
What?

CHODE-A
Give me the ball.

She drops the ball from her vagina and hands it
to him.

He starts to walk away and she lets her guard
down. With a quick turn, he throws the ball full
speed at her-

Without hesitation, she pulls her VAGINA out of
herself and it ignites a gaseous queef blade that
blocks the ball. The vagina handle is bright
pink, and the blade erupts from the vulva. It is
most and beautiful.

REY
Whoa.

CHODE-A
Your friends are in danger. Go now,
you must.

REY
Danger?

                    CHODE-A
          Soon, the Empooper will use the
          Death Shart.

                    REY
          I don't even know where it is.

                    CHODE-A
          Back to where it all started, you
          must look.

She thinks.

                    REY
          Where it all started…

It comes to her. Her eyes widen with fear.

EXT. JOKITCH - DEATH SHART - DAY

The Death Shart is on Jokitch. It has been this whole time. It's a giant butthole on the far side of the planet.

INT. JOKITCH DEATH SHART - HALLWAY - DAY

The Mysterious Man walks along the veiny, red innards of the Death Shart.

A STORMPOOPER SCIENTIST runs up to him.

                    STORMPOOPER SCIENTIST
          Sir, you wanted us to start the
          Death Shart?

                    MYSTERIOUS MAN
          Yes.

                    STORMPOOPER SCIENTIST
          But that will kill everyone on this
          planet.

Mysterious Man glares at him. It puts the
Stormpooper Scientist in a trance.

>   STORMPOOPER SCIENTIST
>   Yes, sir.

Stormpooper Scientist walks away.

>   MYSTERIOUS MAN
>   Soon, we will feed the dark side
>   of the Farts.

INT. ADMIRAL CRAPBAR'S HOME - DAY

Princess Lay-yuh plunges the toilet with her
foot.

>   PRINCESS LAY-YUH
>   Who took a big shit in the toilet?

Finn looks up from the couch.

>   FINN
>   Wasn't me.

Princess Lay-yuh stomps out of the bathroom.

>   PRINCESS LAY-YUH
>   It was probably Jewie with all that
>   shiva food-

She stops dead in her tracks when she sees Rey
standing in front of her.

>   PRINCESS LAY-YUH
>   You're back!

Princess Lay-yuh hugs her, and Finn gets up.

>   FINN
>   Where were you?

                    REY
          With Master Chode-a.

                    PRINCESS LAY-YUH
          You have the Farts, I can feel it.

Rey nods, sheepishly.

                    FINN
          Show me.

Rey focuses, drawing in all her energy…

Then she lets out the biggest queef.

                    PRINCESS LAY-YUH
          My god…

                    FINN
          I knew you had it. It was you all
          along.

                    REY
          You have it too.

                    FINN
          No. I never met Master Chode-a. I
          lied. I'm sorry.

Finn is solemn.

                    REY
          Don't be. We have bigger fish to
          fry. The Empooper is going to
          unleash the Death Shart. It's
          silent, but deadly. It killed my
          boyfriend.

                    FINN
          But we don't even know where it is.

                    REY
          It's here. On Jokitch.

                    PRINCESS LAY-YUH
          We've gotta stop it, but with Jewie
          sitting shiva who will fly the
          Perineum Falcon?

Admiral Crapbar walks up.

                    ADMIRAL CRAPBAR
          I will.

                    REY
          Crapbar. I thought you didn't fight.

                    ADMIRAL CRAPBAR
          Some things are worth farting for.

He dabs her nose with his shitty finger. She goes
to wipe it off but he stops her.

                    ADMIRAL CRAPBAR
          Leave it. Draw strength from it.

                    REY
          It smells really bad.

                    PRINCESS LAY-YUH
          There's no time to waste. How do we
          stop it?

Finn lights up.

                    FINN
          A butt plug.

                    REY
          Perfect. Let's do it.

EXT. JOKITCH - DEATH SHART - DAY

The butthole of the Death Shart puckers.

MILES AWAY

Kylo Ren&Stimpy stumble out of their ship and walk towards the Death Shart.

    STIMPY
 Are we there yet, Ren?

    REN
 Stop with the questions, you idiot!
 Today we destroy the Empooper, and
 get revenge for Shart Vader.

INT./EXT. PERENIUM FALCON

The Perenium Falcon glides through the sky. A butt plug hangs from the bottom.

Admiral Crapbar takes the controls with Princess Lay-yuh. Finn, Rey, and BB-69 sit in the back.

The skies are serene. Too serene as they approach the Death Shart.

    FINN
 This might just be easy.

Admiral Crapbar looks closely at the puckering butthole. Something is coming out of it, ever so slowly. He peers even closer and at the last second realizes what it is-

He spins in his chair-

    ADMIRAL CRAPBAR
 It's a crap!

A large turd flings from the Death Shart at the
Perineum Falcon, followed by a squad of TIE
FARTERS. Within seconds it's an all-out war.

>   REY
> Will you be able to get the butt
> plug in?

>   ADMIRAL CRAPBAR
> We'll need to thin out their numbers.

>   FINN
> I was a gunner in the Empooper.
> I'll handle it.

Finn runs to the gun system in the back, it
shoots cum blasts at the TIE FARTERS.

Finn is absolutely crushing them, and Admiral
Crapbar's prowess as a pilot is unreal.

>   ADMIRAL CRAPBAR
> Are we clear down there?

Rey looks down and sees Kylo Ren&Stimpy enter the
Death Shart. She feels a shudder in her gut. The
same feeling from Dagoballs.

>   REY
> I need to go in there.

>   PRINCESS LAY-YUH
> Why? Kylo Ren&Stimpy will die with
> the blast from the butt plug.

>   REY
> It's not him. It's someone else.

>   PRINCESS LAY-YUH
> Yeah, but that person will die too.
> It'll be fine.

                    REY
          I need to do this. I need to face
          him. Whoever it is.

                    ADMIRAL CRAPBAR
          Be quick. This butt plug won't stay
          lubed forever.

                    REY
          If I'm not back in time, blow it.

                    PRINCESS LAY-YUH
          I can't do that.

                    REY
          You have to. This is bigger than me.

Finn leans down from his gun post.

                    FINN
          She'll make it. I know it.

                    ADMIRAL CRAPBAR
          Go now. We don't have much time.

The Perineum Falcon swoops down near the entrance and Rey does a diving roll out of the hatch.

The dog fight continues as Rey walks into a small crevice entrance on the side to:

INT. DEATH SHART

The sounds of the battle can be heard, muffled, in the Death Shart.

She pulls out her vagina, leaving it unignited.

She creeps through the halls, veiny and red, making her way deeper into the Death Shart.

She reaches the central area. The inner anus. The
air is hazier and dirtier here. It transfixes
her.

Suddenly Kylo Ren&Stimpy's colon almost hits her,
but she ducks in time.

She turns to see him behind her. She ignites her
queef blade.

>   REN
> Ah, so you are the Browneye.

>   REY
> You killed Handjob.

>   REN
> We did what we had to do, to avenge
> Shart Vader.

>   STIMPY
> Are we going to make underleg
> noises, Ren?

Ren hits him.

>   REN
> Shut up and look stupid.

Kylo Ren&Stimpy swings at her, but she's
incredibly good and blocks it.

>   STIMPY
> Let me at her!

They do their classic wrestling over the COLONS
that produces a back and forth battle between
them and Rey.

Rey gets the upper hand, but Ren and Stimply
split up and attack her from both sides.

They circle each other.

> REY
> You're crazy.

> REN
> They all think I'm crazy, but I
> know better. It's not I who are
> crazy. It is I who am mad! Can't
> you hear them? Didn't you see the
> crowd?!

Kylo Ren&Stimpy swing down at her in a barrage that backs her up. She's losing focus, and soon she'll hit the wall with nowhere to go.

The spirit of Handjob Solo appears behind Kylo Ren&Stimpy.

> HANDJOB SOLO
> Use the Farts.

It gives her a renewed sense of vigor. Just about to hit the wall she squeezes her cheeks and lets out a huge, wet butt fart. It stops Kylo Ren&Stimpy in their tracks. Their eyes water.

> REN
> It's so horrible!

They fall to the ground, weeping. They are down and out.

She stands over them, considering giving the final blow.

The Mysterious Man laughs as he walks up to them. She turns her focus to him.

> MYSTERIOUS MAN
> Kill him. Do it. Give in to the
> dark side of the Farts.

She begins to sweat. He has an effect on her.

> REY
> Who are you?

He removes his cloak to reveal-

He is LUKO COCKBLOCKER.

> LUKO COCKBLOCKER
> Rey, I am your father.

EXT./INT. PERINEUM FALCON

The Perineum Falcon swoops up and down, dodging shots.

> ADMIRAL CRAPBAR
> We're almost out of lube. We have to drop it in.

Princess Lay-yuh takes a deep breath.

> PRINCESS LAY-YUH
> Fine. Do it.

The Perineum Falcon drops the butt plug into the Death Shart.

> PRINCESS LAY-YUH
> (gazing out the window)
> Come on, Rey.

INT. DEATH SHART

Luko Cockblocker approaches Rey. Her VAGINA is still aimed at Kylo Ren&Stimpy, as if her body can't move.

> LUKO COCKBLOCKER
> Kill him, Rey. Then join me. Together we will Fart.

                    REY
          I… I can't…

He sneers.

                    LUKO COCKBLOCKER
          Do it!

Her body tenses and she fights off a little queef that grazes Kylo Ren&Stimpy's cheek. His Farts persuasion is powerful.

The Death Shart shudders from the butt plug and starts to fall apart on the inside.

Kylo Ren&Stimpy look weak and pathetic, curled up together.

                    LUKO COCKBLOCKER
          He killed Handjob Solo. Kill him
          Rey. Kill him and I will fart like
          the world has never seen before.

Her eyes narrow at Kylo Ren&Stimpy as she remembers how he had killed Handjob.

She raises her VAGINA up in the air and…

Swings at Luko Cockblocker!

He pulls out his COLON and blocks it, then farts, sending her slamming into the wall.

The structure is falling apart. There isn't much time.

Luko Cockblocker puts his butt cheeks against Rey's face.

                    LUKO COCKBLOCKER
          Now you will die.

We can hear the grumble of a gnarly fart coming-

Kylo Ren&Stimpy's gaseous blade bursts through Luko Cockblocker's stomach. He's saved her.

Luko Cockblocker falls down dead, and Kylo Ren&Stimpy fall to their knees.

Rey comes to his side.

> REY
> Come on. We have to go.

> REN
> Leave us!

> STIMPY
> I'm tired, Ren.

> REN
> (heartfelt)
> Go to sleep, stupid. Go to sleep.

Huge chunks of structure fall.

> REN
> Now go!

Rey nodes and leaves.

Ren holds Stimpy as the building collapses on them.

INT./EXT. PERINEUM FALCON

The TIE FARTERS retreat, sensing the end of the battle.

> ADMIRAL CRAPBAR
> This place is going to blow!

Finn comes to the front of the ship.

>   FINN
>   She'll make it. Just wait.

There's no sign of her as the Death Shart breaks apart. They're going to have to call it…

But she emerges!

>   PRINCESS LAY-YUH
>   There!

Rey waves at them and the Perineum Falcon swoops down to get her.

She gets in the ship and Finn hugs her.

>   FINN
>   I told you you'd make it.

>   ADMIRAL CRAPBAR
>   Hold on to your butts!

The Perineum Falcon flies away as the Death Shart explodes behind them in an eruption of gas.

SLOW FADE TO BLACK

INT. JOKITCH ROOM OF CEREMONIES

Orchestral music blares.

Rey, Finn, Princess Lay-yuh, Admiral Crapbar, and Jewbacca enter a ceremonies room where hundreds of people stand at attention. They walk down the aisle towards Mike O'malley.

>   JEWBACCA
>   Shabbat shalom!

They stand before Mike O'malley so he can bestow
them their honors - a pearl necklace.

He jerks off on each of their chests and they
wear it proudly like a medal.

BB-69 rolls up.

>   BB-69
>   Beep-bloop.

They all smile and look at each other, then Mike
O'malley jerks off on BB-69 as well.

They turn around to face the crowd and bow.

ROLL END CREDITS

Dear reader,

I encourage you to perform this piece in a table read among friends or, if you're feeling particularly ambitious, a staged or filmed production. More importantly, I encourage you to follow your dreams, no matter how stupid they may be.

The only dream not worth pursuing is one that causes pain and suffering.

```
CAST LIST:

CAPTAIN QRUNCH
GENERAL FUCKS
COLLINS
FINN HARDWIPER
REY TOILETBOWLER
BB-69
HANDJOB SOLO
PRINCESS LAY-YUH
JEWBACCA
RANDO COCKJIZZIAN
DOUG FUNNIE
KYLO REN&STIMPY (REN and STIMPY)
MYSTERIOUS MAN/LUKO COCKBLOCKER
ADMIRAL CRAPBAR
MIKE O'MALLEY
OLMEC
STORMPOOPER DIGGER
STORMPOOPER GROUP
STORMPOOPER HELPER
SMALL MAN/CHODE-A
```

About the Author

Joe Cabello is a comedian and writer who is counting on someone else to write the next great American novel so he can focus on writing dumb stories and dad-jokes. You can buy his book *The Longest Haiku* on Amazon, and see his work at the UCB and iO West Theaters in Los Angeles.

Follow on twitter @joecabello
Like his Facebook page
Facebook.com/joecabellowriter
Website: joecabello.com

Printed in Great Britain
by Amazon